REFASHION RESTYLE, RESTITCH

First published in 2022

Search Press Limited
Wellwood, North Farm Road,
Tunbridge Wells, Kent TN2 3DR

Photographs by Garie Hind

Text copyright © Debbie Shore and Kimberley Hind, 2022
Photographs © Garie Hind, 2022
Design copyright © Search Press Ltd. 2022

ISBN: 978-1-78221-993-4
ebook ISBN: 978-1-80093-104-6

The Publishers and author can accept no responsibility for
any consequences arising from the information, advice or
instructions given in this publication. Readers are permitted
to reproduce any of the items/patterns in this book for their
personal use, or for the purpose of selling for charity, free of
charge and without the prior permission of the Publishers.
Any use of the items/patterns for commercial purposes is not
permitted without the prior permission of the Publishers.

For further inspiration:
- visit Debbie's website: www.debbieshoresewing.com
- visit Debbie's YouTube channel:
  www.youtube.com/user/thimblelane
- visit Kimberley's website: www.whatkimberleymakes.com
- visit Kimberley's Instagram page, via @whatkimberleymakes
- join the Half Yard™ Sewing Club: www.halfyardsewingclub.com

SUPPLIERS
For details of suppliers, please visit the Search Press website:
www.searchpress.com

The projects in this book have been made using imperial
measurements, and the metric equivalents provided have been
calculated following standard conversion practices. The imperial
measurements are often rounded to the nearest 5mm for ease
of use except in rare circumstances; however, if you need more
exact measurements, there are a number of excellent online
converters that you can use. Always use either metric or imperial
measurements, not a combination of both.

Dedication

To Vienna, Beatrix and Finn, who are our
family's next generation, and to all future
generations that will hopefully benefit from
the small changes we are making to the
planet today. Who knows, they may well
be refashioning the very clothing you're
wearing now!

REFASHION, RESTYLE, RESTITCH

20 stylish sewing projects from preloved clothes & homewares

DEBBIE SHORE
& KIMBERLEY HIND

SEARCH PRESS

CONTENTS

Tumbling-block Pillow 16

Scallop Lampshade 20

Round Boho Pillow 38

Drawstring
Sweatshirt Bag 42

Reupholstered Footstool 56

Rope Basket 60

Tablecloth Curtains 78

Tie-dye Bean Bag 80

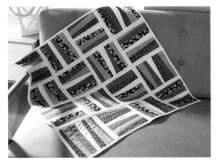

ABOUT THIS BOOK

Many of us nowadays are trying to cut down on waste, particularly fabrics, but may be short of ideas as to how to use those unwanted garments, bedsheets or tablecloths. In this book, we've come up with perhaps unexpected but practical ideas for upcycling and repurposing those items to make like-new home décor and garments that will make you fall in love with your old items over again.

The beauty of working with pre-owned fabrics is that you won't get shrinkage or the risk of colour running, as these items will already have been laundered. You'll also have a wide choice of unique fabrics that you just wouldn't be able to buy new. And, of course, you're keeping that fabric from going to landfill!

To start, take a look in your own wardrobe. What have you not worn for a year or so? Chances are you won't wear it again, but the reason you bought it in the first place was because you loved the fabric, print or colour. How would that sweater look as a pillow cover? Perhaps you've moved house and your curtains are too small; why not use them to cover an old chair or make a bag? Looking at all your neglected clothes and fabrics in this way opens up so many possibilities. You can easily make a start on refashioning your wardrobe without the extra cost of buying items to transform.

We've also explored different techniques in each project – English paper piecing, piping, fitting zips, dyeing and felting – to show the versatility of refashioned fabrics. We hope you'll find them useful when you come up with your own designs and ideas, too.

We understand you won't have or be able to buy the exact fabrics we've used, or may wish to use new fabric from the roll instead of re-purposing; for these reasons, where possible, we've included fabric requirements as well as the materials we've used.

The main thing is to enjoy what you're making, and feel satisfied that you're doing something – no matter how small – to help the environment. Hopefully, we'll inspire you to give it a go!

Debbie
Kym x

▶ Refashioned blinds, pillows and throw

We did a mini makeover with our room with a collection of our refashioned makes! Just look what can be made from old shirts and a duvet cover!

≫ SOURCING FABRICS ≪

We're saying 'sourcing fabrics' as opposed to 'choosing garments' as it's important to look beyond what has been previously constructed. So, although you may normally overlook those Aztec-print palazzo trousers, and may never wear them, just think how amazing that fabric would be for a quilt or a child's dress! That paisley-print shift dress may seem a little old-fashioned, but the fabric would make a fabulous bag lining or a backing on a pillow cover!

▶ Look for vintage clothing, too; you may find something extraordinary and unique, whether it's a 1940s wool suit or a 1960s twist dress!

▶ Some of you will have a project in mind and will source the appropriate fabric to make it; some of you will see a fabric you love then come up with an idea of how to use it. Many of you, like us with this book, will do both! Our mini room make-over (see page 7) started with an idea of what colours we wanted to use, then a trip to a few thrift stores and a look online to choose fabrics.

▶ It's important to consider the purpose of your finished project when choosing fabric. If you're making something that will need washing regularly, then a dry-clean-only garment wouldn't be suitable; if it's a bag or chair cover, you may need a sturdier fabric.

▶ Look closely for wear and tear, too. You may love the print, but if there are worn areas on the fabric you won't be able to use it. Be aware of darts, pockets and seams that will prevent you from cutting an area of fabric to the size that you want. For instance, a man's shirt will have no bust darts but may have darts in the front and/or back at the waist; a ladies' blouse may have bust and waist darts.

▶ Look beyond the fabric! Buttons, buckles, bag fastenings, zips and hardware can be expensive to buy new, but on used items it's not unusual to find a few real gems, even if you're not fond of the items they came from.

▶ **Our favourite transformations**

Top to bottom:
turning a wool scarf into felted mittens;
refashioning a tasselled dress into a
lampshade; and taking apart jackets to
create a sophisticated tweed bag!

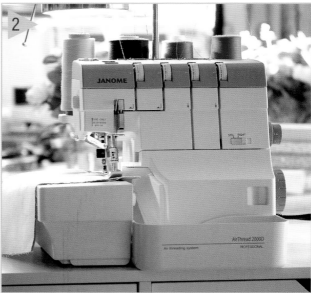

≫ SEWING KIT ≪

1 Sewing machine

The projects in this book can be made on any sewing machine, as straight and zigzag stitches are all you'll need. However, a basic sewing machine may struggle with thick fabrics. If you're in the market for an upgrade, we suggest a computerized machine; they are easy to use and generally have a vast range of stitches.

2 Overlocker/serger

Not a necessity, but an overlocker/serger sews in super-quick time, finishes seams effortlessly and is ideal if you're working with stretch fabrics.

3 Thread

Using strong, good-quality thread is important for strong seams. Nowadays, recycled thread made from plastic bottles is also available, so you can make your refashioned items even more sustainable!

4 Dressmaking shears

Scissors with long blades and comfortable handles are ideal, making light work of thicker fabrics and seams as you prepare your garments for their transformation.

5 Snips

These are small, pointed scissors that allow you to snip into stitches without damaging the fabric.

6 Quick unpick/seam ripper

You'll be doing a lot of unpicking, so invest in a few of these as they'll blunt after a while!

7 Hand-sewing needles

We've used these for invisible sewing, gathering and closures, so you'll need these. We like to use sharps that have a small round head and slip through the fabric easily.

8 Tape measure

A tape measure is a sewing room essential whether you're dressmaking or making homewares. Replace fabric tape measures regularly as these can stretch over time.

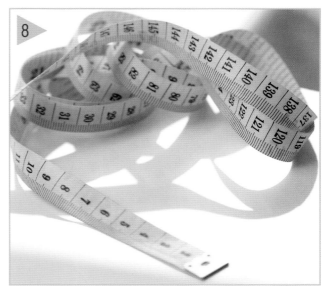

9 Rotary cutter, ruler and cutting mat

The most-used size of rotary cutter in this book is 45mm (1¾in). Although rotary cutters work with rulers to make straight-line cutting a breeze, free-hand cutting around curves is easier than you may think. Be careful of the blades – they are incredibly sharp! Rulers come in all shapes and sizes. If you're just buying one, we suggest a 15.25 x 61cm (6 x 24in) one with 45-degree lines so that you can also cut on the bias. With the cutting mat, go for the biggest one you can find or afford!

10 Thimble

Thimbles are useful, particularly for techniques that involve hand sewing like English paper piecing and smocking – you'll need help to protect your fingers from the end of the needle when you're pushing it repeatedly through fabric.

11 Interfacing and wadding/batting

Synthetic, natural or a combination of both, the choice is yours! Waddings/battings add 'padding' to your project and are perfect for quilting. Fusible interfacing is useful to prevent stretch fabrics from stretching, as we used in our Round Boho Pillow (see page 38), or to add stability to fine fabrics. Foam is thicker and is perfect to add sturdiness to a bag such as the Tweed Tote (see page 32).

12 Adhesives

We recommend a repositionable spray adhesive to secure appliqué pieces or to bond wadding/batting to your fabric. A strong wet fabric glue is important for gluing in some features (see the Reupholstered Footstool on page 56). A dot of glue behind a zip can help keep it secured while you sew it in place.

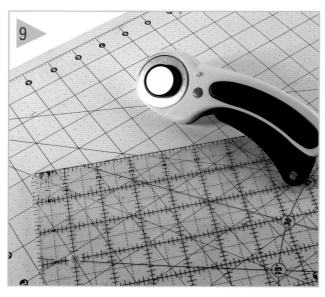

13 Marking pens

You can choose from a range of heat-, water- or air-erasable pens, but be careful not to iron over water- or air-erasable types as the ink will set and become permanent. We tend to use heat-erasable pens; however, always test on a patch of scrap fabric first as the ink can fade the print on some fabrics.

14 Pins

Flower- or glass-head pins are handy as they're much more visible in the fabric and on the floor when they're inevitably dropped!

15 Fabric clips

Clips are a great alternative for holding together thicker fabrics that can't be pinned.

16 Iron

Although we mostly use a steam iron for pressing the projects, a little travel iron next to the sewing machine is useful for a quick pressing.

≫ GOOD TO KNOW ≪

MACHINE STITCHES

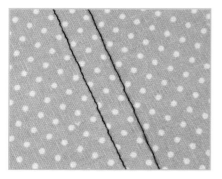

Straight stitch

This is the most-used stitch in any project. Lengthen the thread to create a tacking/basting stitch and, if you loosen the tension, it's easy to pull the bottom thread to gather your fabric.

Zigzag stitch

A decorative stitch that can be used to join two pieces of fabric together to create a flat seam or around the edge of appliqué. This stitch can also be useful to help stop the raw edges of your fabric from fraying if you don't have an overlocker/serger.

Over-edge stitch

This is designed to take the thread slightly over the raw edge of your fabric to stop it from fraying (it is similar to an overlock stitch, which is produced by an overlocker/serger). Use this on items that may wear or need to be laundered; if you sell your items this will give them a professional finish.

HAND STITCHES

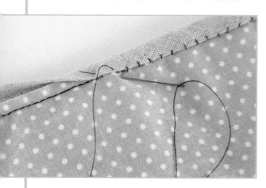

Slip stitch

Keep the stitch to a short length and try to catch just a couple of strands of the fold or edge of the fabric to keep the stitch as invisible as possible.

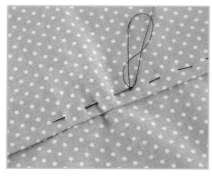

Running stitch

Use this in the same way as a machine straight stitch (if tiny, the stitches can be just as strong). It can be used as a tacking/basting stitch, and the stitches can be pulled to gather the fabric, as on the Round Boho Pillow (see page 38).

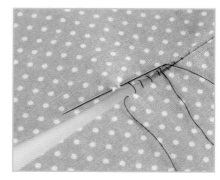

Ladder stitch

The perfect stitch for closing turning gaps or making repairs in seams: take the needle from one side of the opening to the opposite side, then gently pull to close the gap. Small stitches in matching thread are the least visible.

INSERTING A ZIP INTO A SEAM

Zips aren't as daunting as many people think, so don't be afraid to work with them! There are many ways to insert a zip into your project, but we find this method the easiest, especially for pillow covers. We've used it for the Tie-Dye Beanbag on page 80.

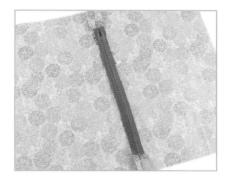

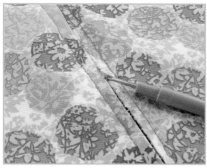

1 Allow for a 1.25cm (½in) seam where the zip will be inserted. Press the seam open. Place your zip facing downwards and secure temporarily with fabric glue or tacking/basting stitches.

2 Sew a box shape around the zip, sewing from the right side to ensure a neat stitch line. Unpick the stitches over the teeth of the zip with a quick unpick.

PIPING

Piping adds a touch of class to any project, and although you can buy pre-made piping, you'll always have the right colour if you make your own. Cord comes in many different sizes, but we tend to use a cord up to 5mm (¼in) wide.

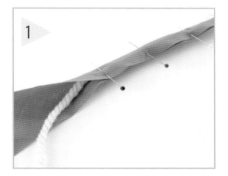

1 Cut your fabric into strips, wide enough to wrap around the cord plus a good 5mm (¼in) to go under the sewing machine needle. If you're taking the piping around curves and corners, then cut the fabric strips on the bias. Pin the raw edges together, sandwiching the cord in the centre.

2 Using the zipper foot on your machine, sew alongside the cord, making sure the raw fabric edges are together. Take out the pins as you sew.

3 To apply the piping to your fabric, pin it right sides and raw edges together, then sew with your zipper foot. Keep your needle close to the cord without actually sewing through it.

4 When using piping as an edging between two pieces of fabric, align the piping as in step 3 and then pin the second piece of fabric right side down on top. Stitch in place and turn out.

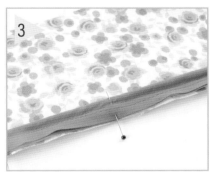

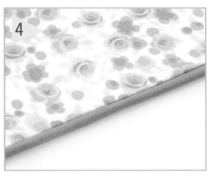

Tip

To join the ends of piping, at one end trim the piping cord inside the fabric by about 2.5cm (1in) then fold over the end of the fabric by 6mm (¼in). Tuck the other (untrimmed) end of the piping cord inside the folded end then sew along the joined piping edge as normal.

TUMBLING-BLOCK PILLOW

English paper piecing (EPP) is a relaxing hand-sewing pastime. It's not a quick technique; the small area on this pillow cover took three evenings to complete. But, of all the EPP designs out there, this one, known as the Tumbling Block, has the most striking, three-dimensional effect! The key is to choose three contrasting fabrics in light, medium and dark tones to create the effect of light reflecting on cubes.

Choose fabrics that are 100 per cent woven cotton, as you'll need them to crease well and not distort. The three shirts we bought from a charity/thrift/op store were ideal, and there was plenty of fabric left over to make a second pillow cover (see page 88). We also used some of the leftover striped fabric from the trousers used for the patchwork throw (see page 24) on the back of the pillow.

We've used a rectangular pillow pad, but this would work well with any shape of pad; just keep adding diamonds – above, below or to the sides – until you reach the size you need.

Made from

Three shirts, one pair of trousers

FINISHED SIZE

40.5 x 30.5cm (16 x 12in)

YOU WILL NEED

▶ 56 x 30.5cm (22 x 12in) light coloured fabric – we used a pale shirt

▶ 56cm (22in) square of medium coloured fabric – we used a striped mid-blue shirt

▶ 61 x 53.5cm (24 x 21in) dark fabric – we used a plain dark-navy shirt

▶ Tumbling Block template (see page 96) and paper, for the pattern pieces

▶ 25.5 x 33cm (10 x 13in) coordinating fabric, for the envelope back (or you will have enough fabric from the three pieces above to join together to make this back piece, if you wish) – we used a pair of trousers

▶ Fabric glue pen

▶ Hand-sewing needle and strong thread

▶ 40.5 x 30.5cm (16 x 12in) pillow pad

NOTE

Use a 5mm (¼in) seam allowance

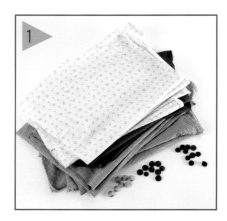

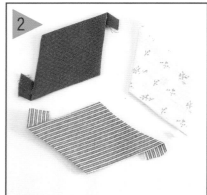

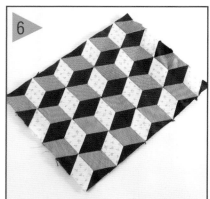

1 Carefully cut your shirts into large fabric pieces, removing any seams, collars, cuffs, pockets and plackets. And remember to save the buttons!

2 Trace off the template and cut out as many paper tumbling blocks as required. You will need 25 dark, 18 light and 18 medium colours for the panel shown here (so a total of 61 paper diamonds). Pin these to your fabrics, then cut the fabric 5mm (¼in) larger than the paper pieces. Centre one paper diamond over the wrong side of one fabric piece and glue around the edge. Fold the fabric around the paper. Don't trim off the points; these will help the pieces to nest together later. Repeat with the remaining fabric and paper pieces.

3 Place a light- and medium-coloured fabric piece right sides together and join them along one side with an over-edge stitch, such as whip stitch. Keep your stitches small and close together, just catching a couple of threads over the edge of the fabric. Don't worry if you catch the paper piece occasionally. When you come to the end make sure you knot tightly before cutting the thread.

4 Open out the pieces. Sew the third, dark-coloured diamond in place along two edges. You will need to fold one of the diamonds as you come to the 'Y' seam in the centre. Now you've completed the first block! From the right side of the diamonds, your stitches should be barely visible.

5 Create 16 blocks in the same way, and sew them all together in rows. Offer your patchwork to the pillow pad to make sure you've covered most of one side – remember, you'll be adding a fabric border. If you need to add more diamonds around the edge to increase the size or change the shape, then do so now.

6 Trim the block to straighten the edges and to measure 35.5 x 28cm (14 x 11in). Press, then carefully remove the paper pieces. If the glue is a little firm, use a warm iron to help soften it as you remove the pieces.

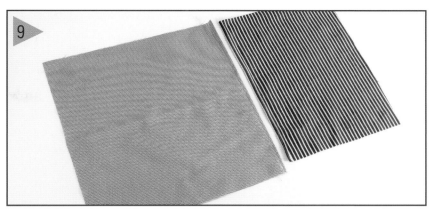

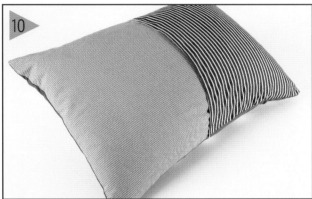

7 Cut two strips of dark fabric, each measuring 6.5 x 28cm (2½ x 11in). Sew a strip to each side of the tumbling block, right sides together, using a 5mm (¼in) seam allowance.

8 Cut two 6.5 x 46cm (2½ x 18in) strips of dark fabric, then sew these right sides together to the top and bottom of the panel. Trim the panel to measure 42 x 32cm (16½ x 12½in).

9 For the back of the pillow cover, cut one piece of medium fabric measuring 28 x 32cm (11 x 12½in), and one from the contrasting fabric measuring 23 x 32cm (9 x 12½in). Fold over one 32cm (12½in) edge of each piece to the wrong side twice by 5mm (¼in), then sew to hem.

10 Place the contrast piece over the front of the cushion cover, right sides together, matching the raw edges and with the hemmed edge in the middle. Repeat with the medium-coloured piece, again with the right side facing down. The hemmed edges should overlap at the centre. Sew all the way around the cover with a 5mm (¼in) seam allowance. Turn the cover right side out and insert your pillow pad. Here's the pillow from the back...

11 ... and here it is from the front!

SCALLOP LAMPSHADE

This lampshade can be made using many different types of fabric. If you choose a stretch fabric, you'll have more give when fitting the cover onto the frame. If it's a woven fabric that you want to use, make sure you cut out the panels on the bias; this will add some stretch to the fabric. If you have enough fabric to fussy cut the design, then do so. This will give the lamp a professional finish, especially if it's a larger print. Small, busy designs will be more forgiving.

We found a polycotton crinkled dress with fringing, which was ideal for our lampshade design, although the fringe needed re-knotting and mending in places!

Frames can be bought new, but you can find many different shapes in charity/thrift/op stores too.

Made from

One beach dress

FINISHED SIZE

43.5cm (17in) square

YOU WILL NEED

▶ Scallop lampshade frame –
ours measured 101.5cm (40in) in circumference, 25.5cm (10in) deep

▶ 81.5 x 30.5cm (32 x 12in) fabric –
allow more for fussy cutting

▶ Strong double-sided adhesive tape

▶ Pillow pad

▶ Erasable marker pen

▶ Scrap piece of fabric measuring approx.
23 x 30.5cm (9 x 12in), for the template –
using a light fabric that is transparent can help if you're fussy cutting

▶ Optional: pinking shears; fringing or braids and textile glue, for the trim

NOTE

Use a 5mm (¼in) seam allowance

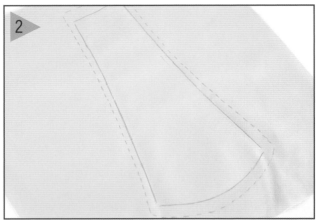

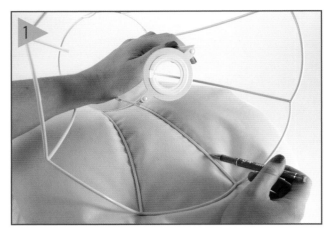

Tip

You can use paper to create the template if you'd prefer, although fabric is slightly easier as it can form around the cushion pad and frame.

1 To make a template, lay a scrap piece of fabric over a pillow pad that is larger than the lampshade you're covering. Push the lampshade on top of the fabric to create an indent in the pillow. Using an erasable pen, draw the shape of the panel onto the fabric. (You need to draw around the outside of the frame panel.)

2 Add 2.5cm (1in) to the top and bottom of the template. This will allow for the fabric to tuck around the frame. Add a 5mm (¼in) seam allowance to either side of the template. Cut the template out.

3 Cut away any seams, fastenings and trims from your garment. Use the template to cut out the panels of your lampshade. We needed eight panels, and decided to fussy cut the fabric.

Tip

Don't throw the template away. After completing step 6, you could make a little girl's skirt out of the lampshade panels instead! To do this, fold the top of the circle over twice and thread elastic through. Hem the bottom edge by folding over twice.

Light bulbs

We'd recommend using a low wattage, energy-efficient light bulb as this produces minimum heat.

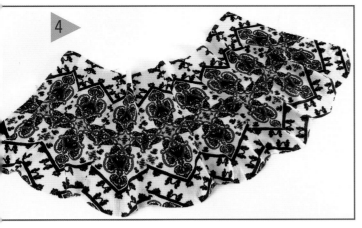

4 Sew the first panel right sides together to the second. Open and press. Continue to join the remaining panels in this way.

5 Sew the two remaining edges right sides together to create a tube.

6 Slip the tube over the lampshade frame. It needs to be a snug fit; if it isn't, go back and re-sew the seams with a larger seam allowance. Once the cover fits the lampshade, you can use pinking shears to neaten the seams. Make sure the seams of the panels are in line with the panels of the frame. Stick the strong adhesive tape all around the bottom edge of the frame, on the inside. Start to pull the fabric taut around the bottom edge of the frame and stick in place, as shown. Continue to do this until all panels are secure, making sure the seams are still in the right place.

7 Repeat with the top of the frame. Once you are happy with the placement, tuck the fabric under the frame to neaten. If you have any trims to add (such as our fringing), use a textile glue to adhere it to the lampshade. Make sure to overlap the ends of the trim to prevent them from fraying.

PATCHWORK THROW

This is the throw for the impatient, those new to quilting or those who just can't make points meet! The Quilt As You Go (QAYG) technique is also ideal if you lack space to sew in, as each block is quilted separately before making it up.

We've used monochrome fabric from a pair of trousers, a skirt and a dress, with a tinge of colour from a blue shirt and, to break up the patterns, a white blouse. There is plenty of fabric left over for many more makes – as you'll see on the following pages. We've used one white strip along the centre of each block to give the blocks a bit of uniformity.

Woven cotton is the ideal fabric for patching. Our long dress was crinkled so we added fusible interfacing to the wrong side to prevent it from stretching, but to also keep the crinkles for texture.

Made from

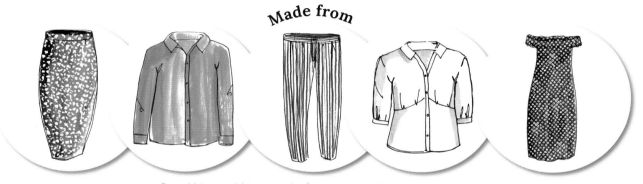

One skirt, one shirt, one pair of trousers, one blouse, one dress

FINISHED SIZE

81.5cm (32in) square

YOU WILL NEED

The measurements are for the materials we've used; of course, you can change these if you use more or fewer prints and colours.

- ▶ 112 x 127cm (44 x 50in) white fabric
- ▶ 111 x 25.5cm (40 x 10in) blue fabric
- ▶ 111 x 51cm (40 x 20in) striped fabric
- ▶ 111 x 41cm (40 x 16in) floral fabric
- ▶ 11 x 51cm (40 x 20in) crinkle fabric
- ▶ 90cm (35in) square of wadding/batting, cut into sixteen 20.5cm (8in) squares
- ▶ Tacking/basting spray

NOTE

Use a 5mm (¼in) seam allowance

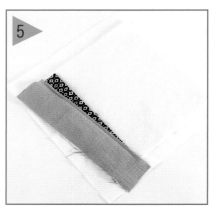

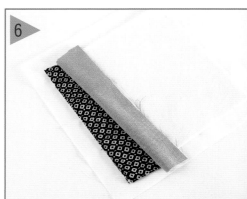

1 Carefully cut away the seams of your garments. Save any fastenings, such as buttons, for future projects.

2 Cut some of the fabric into 5cm (2in) wide strips. It's a good idea to cut too little and add more strips if you need to, than cut too many and have strips left over. We used approximately seven strips for each block, which means we cut around 112 strips overall. Don't worry about the strips varying in width slightly; this only adds to the quilt's improvised appearance!

3 Cut sixteen 25.5cm (10in) squares of white fabric. Spray the wrong sides of each wadding/batting square with tacking/basting spray and place one centrally to the wrong side of each white square.

4 Place one strip of fabric right side up over the left side of a wadding/batting square and trim to the same length. Sew along the long outside edge to secure. Start and stop sewing 5mm (¼in) from each end of the wadding/batting.

5 Place a second strip right side down over the first, at an angle, covering the long raw edge of the first piece. Trim the strip to measure slightly longer than the length of the wadding/batting. Sew along the right edge, starting and stopping 5mm (¼in) from the edge of the wadding/batting.

6 Fold the strip to the right side and press.

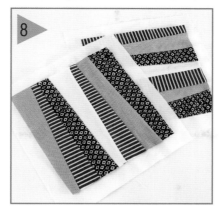

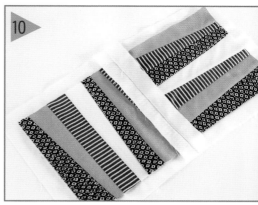

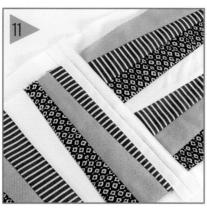

7 Continue in the same way, alternating the angle of each strip, until the whole square of wadding/batting is covered.

8 Fold the backing fabric away from the quilted area then trim the strips to the same size as the wadding/batting. (This is why you started and stopped sewing 5mm (¼in) from each side of the wadding/batting.)

9 Repeat with all the blocks.

10 Take two blocks and place them wrong sides together (the patchwork pieces facing outwards), with the strips facing at right angles. Sew the two blocks together along one side, close to the edge of the wadding/batting. Press the seam open.

11 Fold the edges of each seam allowance over by 1.25cm (½in) and press. Topstitch along the edges of the folds. This creates a 'bound' look along the seam.

12 Repeat until you have a row of four blocks. At this point don't fold the top, bottom or outer sides.

13 Make up another row in the same way and sew it toget. Sew one row wrong sides together to the first, again along the edge of the wadding/batting. Press the seam open. Fold the edges under by 1.25cm (½in) and press. Topstitch in place.

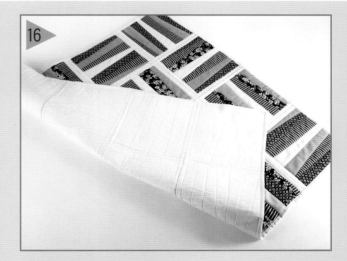

14 Make and add two rows in the same way.

15 Fold the outside edges to the right side of the quilt by 1.25cm (½in) and press. Mitre the corners as you go.

16 Topstitch all the way round. Your quilt is now backed, quilted and bound!

ROLL-UP BLIND

This blind was made from one double duvet cover, and there was even a little fabric to spare. As the fabric was quite a lightweight cotton it makes a pretty window dressing, but may not be too practical in keeping out the light!

The curtain pole is extendable and fits within the window recess without the need to be screwed into the frame. These are available to buy from most hardware stores and are very easy to fit.

Your fabric requirements depend on the size of your window; our measurements are based on this 91.5 x 116.75cm (36 x 46in) window frame.

Made from

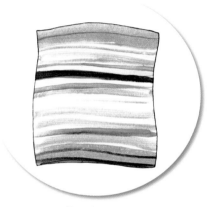

Duvet cover

FINISHED SIZE

91.5 x 117cm (36 x 46in)

YOU WILL NEED

► Double-bed duvet cover, or 229 x 279.5cm (90 x 110in) of striped fabric – this allowed us to cut out and make stripes in different directions; if you are using plain fabrics, you will need less fabric

► Extendable curtain pole that extends to 91.5cm (36in) in length

NOTE

Use a 1.25cm (½in) seam allowance

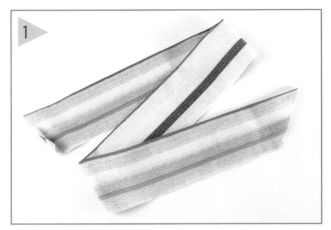

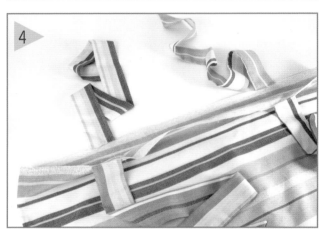

1 Begin with the ties. Cut four strips of fabric, each measuring 18 x 91.5cm (7 x 36in). Fold each one in half lengthways, right sides together. Cut across one end at a 45-degree angle.

2 Sew along the long and angled sides of each strip, leaving the short straight side open. Trim the seam allowances across the points, turn the strips right side out and press.

3 For the main blind, cut two pieces of fabric each measuring 94 x 104.5cm (37 x 41in). Sew two ties to the top of each piece, 13cm (5in) in from each side, raw edges matching and the angled end facing downwards.

4 Sew the two large pieces right sides together, leaving the top open. Be careful not to sew over the ends of the ties! Snip across the seam allowances at the corners and then turn the blind right side out.

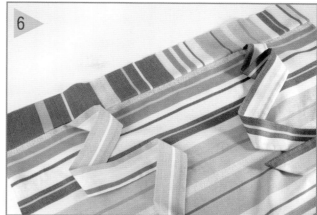

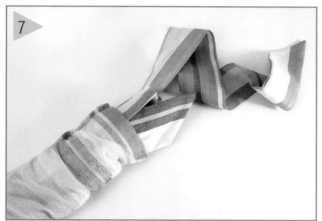

5 For the blind top, cut two large strips of fabric, each measuring 94 x 18cm (37 x 7in). Fold the short ends over to the wrong sides by 1.25cm (½in) and press.

6 Place the strips across the top of each side of the main blind panel, right sides together, and sew both in place in one go, close to the previous stitching. Fold back the strips and press.

7 Tightly roll up the whole of the curtain blind (including the ties), starting from the bottom until the top edges of the curtain meet, right sides together. Sew across the top of the curtain, taking care to avoid catching any extra fabric in the seam as you stitch.

8 Pull the fabric through the tube to turn the whole blind right side out. Press. Topstitch all around the edge, leaving a 4cm (1½in) gap at each side of the top channel to thread the pole through.

9 Insert your pole into the window recess, following the manufacturer's instructions. Roll the blind up and tie it in place, then step back and admire your work!

Tip

You could use a heavier fabric for your window blind, or line it with blackout lining. However, you may have to increase the length of the main blind pieces to allow room for the rolling!

TWEED TOTE

This bag is made from two tweed jackets we found in a thrift/charity/op shop, which we chose because the fabrics worked well together.

There are a few things to bear in mind before starting to work with loosely woven material. In particular, look at the elbows or, if using trousers or skirts, the knees and seat – loose weaves can stretch around these areas, so will be unusable. The lining from the red jacket was unusable, but we managed to find a pair of red pillowcases that matched perfectly!

Bear in mind that fitted garments tend to have lots of darts which you'll need to cut around. Tweed fabric may twist as you sew, so you will need some form of stabilizer if you use this type of fabric.

Made from

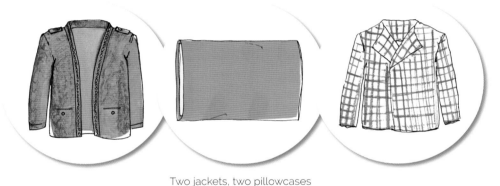

Two jackets, two pillowcases

FINISHED SIZE

38 x 28 x 9cm (15 x 11 x 3½in)

YOU WILL NEED

▶ 102 x 41cm (40 x 16in) fabric for the front, back, inner flap and strap – we used the red jacket

▶ 61 x 43.5cm (24 x 17in) contrast fabric for the sides, base, outer flap and inner pocket fabric – we used the checked jacket

▶ 112 x 46cm (44 x 18in) coordinating fabric for the lining – we used old pillowcases

▶ 112 x 46cm (44 x 18in) piece of single-sided fusible foam stabilizer

▶ Two magnetic snaps

▶ Trims, buttons and design features for fastening and decorating the bag – we used the trims from the red jacket, plus the buttoned epaulettes

NOTE

Use a 1.25cm (½in) seam allowance

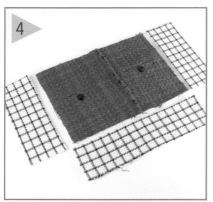

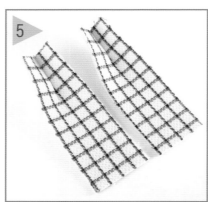

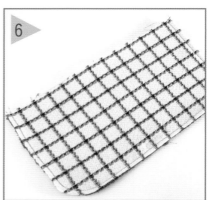

1 Cut along the seams of the jackets, and remove any hardware and trims.

2 To create a piece of fabric large enough for the front of the bag, sew the two front jacket pieces together. The pockets are faux, but we liked the look so kept them!

3 Cut a 41 x 30.5cm (16 x 12in) rectangle from the joined red jacket front. Cut another from the back of the jacket. Fuse foam to the wrong sides of both pieces.

4 Cut two pieces of contrast fabric each measuring 10 x 30.5cm (4 x 12in) for the sides, and one for the base measuring 41 x 10cm (16 x 4in). Fuse foam to the wrong sides.

5 Fold the side sections in half lengthways and sew 5cm (2in) along the fold.

6 Cut two pieces of fabric, one from each jacket, measuring 33 x 20.5cm (13 x 8in) for the flap. Curve the bottom two corners – you can use a small plate as a template if you wish. Fuse foam to the wrong side of the outer flap piece (ours is the checked jacket). Then, sew the two flap pieces right sides together, leaving the top straight edge open. Trim the foam back to the seam allowance, turn the right side out and press. Edge stitch around the seam.

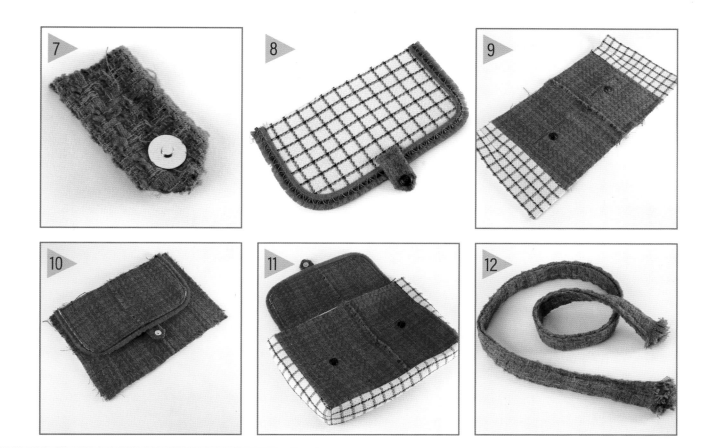

7 Attach the thinner part of a magnetic snap to the pointed end of the epaulette, as shown, or make a fastener strip as follows. Cut two strips of fabric measuring 8 x 9cm (3 x 3½in), pin them right sides together and trim one end to a point. Stitch the long edges and pointed end, trim the seam allowances at the angles and turn right side out.

8 Sew the decorative trim around the bottom three sides of the outer flap. Fold the raw edge of the fastener strip or epaulette under by 5mm (¼in) then sew it to the centre-bottom of the flap, the magnetic snap facing down, and tucking away any raw edges.

9 Sew the sides of the bag right sides together to the front.

10 Sew the flap right sides together to the centre-top of the back of the bag.

11 With right sides together, sew the back to the sides of the bag then sew in the base. Turn the bag right side out.

12 To make the strap, cut a length of fabric measuring 46 x 10cm (18 x 4in). We needed to join two strips to achieve this length, but managed to leave a fringe on each end. If you have no fringe, turn the short ends under by 1.25cm (½in) and press. Fold the two long sides to the centre, the fabric wrong sides together, then fold the whole piece in half and press. Topstitch along each side.

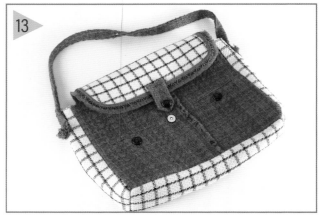

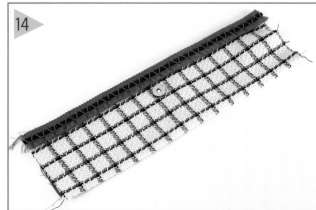

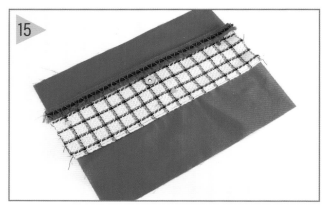

13 Sew the strap to each side of the bag, 2.5cm (1in) from the top. Fold the flap over and mark the position of the thicker half of the magnetic snap; make sure it's central to the front of the bag. Attach the snap, following the manufacturer's instructions.

14 For the inside pocket, cut two lengths of fabric – one from outer and one from lining – each measuring 41 x 15.5cm (16 x 6in). Apply the thicker part of a magnetic snap to the centre-front of the outer (white) fabric, 2.5cm (1in) from the top. Sew the outer and lining pocket pieces right sides together across the top and bottom, then turn the right side out. Add a length of trim to the top of the pocket.

15 For the lining, cut two pieces of fabric each measuring 41 x 30.5cm (16 x 12in), two measuring 10 x 30.5cm (4 x 12in) and one measuring 41 x 10cm (16 x 4in). Place the pocket over one 41 x 30.5cm (16 x 12in), 7.5cm (3in) from the top. Sew across the bottom and sides, then add a couple of dividing lines to separate the pockets. These can be anywhere across the pocket you like: closer together for pens, wider for a mobile/cell phone.

16 We used the second epaulette as a pocket fastening, with the thinner side of the magnetic snap on the back, but you can make a fastener yourself as described in step 7 on page 35. Turn in the raw fabric at the end if necessary, then match the two sides of the snap then sew the fastening in place.

17 Sew the front, back, sides and base of the lining right sides together in the same way as the outer bag, this time leave a turning gap in one base seam of about 15.5cm (6in).

18 Push the bag inside the lining, right sides together, matching the seams. Sew around the top.

19 Turn the bag right side out. If your foam is crinkled, then give the bag a blast of steam from your iron. Sew the opening in the lining closed, then push the lining inside the bag. Edge stitch around the top.

Tip

When sewing thick fabrics, a denim needle may help. These needles are strong and are designed to cope with multiple layers of heavy fabrics, not just denim!

ROUND BOHO PILLOW

We loved the colour combination and textures of this jersey sweater and polyester skirt. Although stretch fabric wouldn't seem ideal for homewares, fusing lightweight interfacing to the wrong side stopped any stretch and made the fabric much easier to work with. The tied centre is an unusual feature and gives our cushion a relaxed, comfy look!

Made from

One jersey sweater, one wrap skirt

FINISHED SIZE

40.5cm (16in) in diameter

YOU WILL NEED

- ► 40.5cm (16in) diameter round pillow pad
- ► Four pieces of fabric – two in one colour, two in the other – each measuring 33cm (13in) wide x 43.5cm (17in) long
- ► 40.5 x 7.5cm (16 x 3in) of fabric for the tie – we used the sweater fabric
- ► Optional: 132 x 43.5cm (52 x 17in) fusible interfacing (if using stretch fabric)

NOTE

Use a 1.25cm (½in) seam allowance

1 Fuse interfacing to the wrong sides of the fabric panels, if you are using stretch fabric. Sew the pieces right sides together along the longer sides, alternating the colours of the panels.

2 Sew the long ends together to form a tube.

3 Turn the raw edges of the top and bottom ends over by 1.25cm (½in) and sew to make a hem. Slip the tube over your pillow pad to ensure the fit is snug – you can always increase the seam allowance to make it tighter, if necessary. Bring the free ends together, over the centre of the pillow. Work a running stitch by hand across the edge of one panel (here, the bottom orange-red one), pulling the thread tight to gather.

4 Repeat with the opposite panel (here, the hemmed edge of the top orange-red one). Then sew the two gathered pieces together in the centre of the cushion.

5 Gather the other two panels in the same way (here, the patterned fabric), and sew together over the top of the first panels. Repeat with the second side of your cushion cover.

6 To make the tie for the pillow front, fold the strip of fabric in half lengthways then sew right sides together, making a 45-degree angle at each end and leaving a turning gap in the side of about 5cm (2in). Turn the tie right side out and then sew the opening closed.

7 Thread the tie under the gathered top fabric of the pillow front and knot to finish.

DRAWSTRING SWEATSHIRT BAG

Use a kid's sweatshirt to make a handy drawstring bag for toys, crayons or any other bits and bobs! Using the ribbing from the bottom of the sweatshirt is a quick and easy way to finish off the bag!

Made from

Child's sweatshirt

FINISHED SIZE

25.5 x 28cm (10 x 11in)

YOU WILL NEED

▶ Small sweatshirt – ours was size 2–3 years

▶ 61cm (24in) length of 1.25cm (½in) wide ribbon or string

▶ Safety pin or bodkin, for threading the ribbon

▶ Rotary cutter and cutting mat

NOTE

Use a 5mm (¼in) seam allowance

1

2

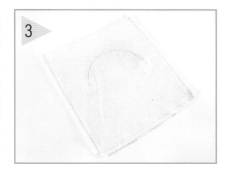
3

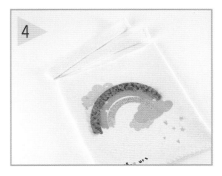
4

5

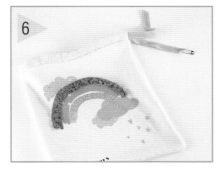
6

1 Cut the arms and bottom ribbing off the sweatshirt.

2 With the front and back of the sweatshirt still intact, cut out a rectangle shape as large as you can through both fabric layers.

3 Sew the front and back pieces right sided together around the sides and bottom, leaving the top edge open. Cut off the the corners of the seam allowances at the bottom to reduce bulk, making sure not to cut through any stitches, as shown. Turn the bag right side out and push out the corners.

4 Cut the ribbing band so that you have one long strip of fabric. Fold the strip in half widthways and sew the two ends closed, adjusting the seam allowance so that the band will fit the top of your bag.

5 Sew the fabric strip right sides together to the bag, leaving a small gap at the start and end to insert the ribbon.

6 Attach a safety pin to the end of the ribbon then thread the ribbon through the ribbing-band channel and out the other side. Tie the ends of the ribbon in a knot. Pull tight to draw the bag closed.

FELT MITTENS

Many of us will have accidentally shrunk and felted a sweater by washing at too high a temperature, then experienced the disappointment of ruining a favourite (and usually expensive!) garment. However, that now matted, small item can be transformed into many projects, from mittens to hot-water bottles, and much more!

When wool is felted it binds the fibres closely together and creates fabric that doesn't fray. How much your sweater will shrink and how thick it will eventually be is an unknown entity, and is one of the most fun parts of the whole process!

When upcycling a garment to felt, look for one made from at least 80 per cent pure wool. Men's sweaters are generally larger than women's, so using these means you'll have more fabric to play with. If you're felting a few items, don't mix the colours as shedded lint tends to stick and can spoil the look of your felt. If you're only felting one or two items, it would be worth adding something like an old pair of jeans to help with the tumbling motion. After washing, tumble-dry the garment – it may shrink and felt even more! Make sure to remove any fastenings like zips and buttons before washing and drying.

Made from

Woollen scarf

FINISHED SIZE

Each glove approx. 17.75 x 25.5cm (7 x 10in), depending on the size of your hands

YOU WILL NEED

▶ Garment or accessory made from at least 80 per cent wool, with an area of fabric at least 30.5 x 76.5cm (12 x 30in) in size – we used an old scarf

▶ Paper and pencil, for making a template

▶ Wool or tapestry needle

▶ Ball of wool, for sewing with (this means it shouldn't be too chunky!)

1 Place the wool garment or accessory in your washing machine with a small amount of detergent and wash it at around 60°C (140°F). Once the cycle is over, chuck it in the tumble-dryer until dry. After washing, our scarf shrunk by about half! The colour also softened a little after felting.

2 As we used a scarf we cut away the fringes, leaving 2.5cm (1in) of felted fabric above to create a useable trim for later!

3 Make a template for your mittens by drawing around your hand using the paper and pencil. Keep your fingers closed when you do this, and add 2.5cm (1in) below the hand to make the wrist opening. Once the main outline is complete, add a 2.5cm (1in) seam allowance all around.

4 Use your template to cut four mitten shapes from your garment or accessory. If your fabric has a right and wrong side, make sure two of the mitten shapes are mirror-imaged.

5 Using the wool or tapestry needle and the ball of wool, hand sew the shapes together in pairs with an over-edge stitch, such as whip stitch. Make the stitches about 5mm (¼in) apart and remember to leave the wrist open!

— Tip —

What to do with those left-over pieces? Make them into tumble-dryer balls!

First, cut as many 13cm (5in) circles as you can – don't worry about them being perfectly round. Work running stitch around the edge, then pull the thread slightly to gather. Cut the remaining felted scraps into smaller pieces and place these inside the circle. Gather the top of the circle and sew over to secure. Soak the balls in a mixture of white vinegar, water and a few drops of your favourite essential oil for beautifully fragranced laundry!

6 Repeat with the second pair.

7 We added the leftover fringing to the bottom edges of the wrist opening on each mitten, again using an over-edge stitch.

8 Your mittens are ready to wear!

HOT-WATER BOTTLE COVER
& CHILDREN'S LEGWARMERS

We couldn't resist buying this rainbow-striped child's sweater when we saw it in a charity/thrift/op shop. And what to do with the leftover sleeves? Make legwarmers, of course!

These are simple projects that could easily be sewn by hand, and could be a great introduction for children into the world of sewing and upcycling.

Made from

One child's knitted sweater

Tips for sewing with knits

► Always finish the seams on knitwear as it will unravel easily! Jersey knits, on the other hand, don't fray so won't need finishing.

► Use a ballpoint needle – these needles have a slightly rounded tip, so won't break the yarn of the fabric when sewing.

► Be careful not to stretch the seams as you're sewing, as this could cause the seam to ripple.

FINISHED SIZES

Hot-water bottle: 20.5 x 29.5cm (8 x 11½in)

Legwarmers: depends on the length of the sleeve and the size of the child; ours measured 33cm (13in) in length

YOU WILL NEED

► Child's sweater or two 23 x 30.5cm (9 x 12in) pieces of knitted fabric, plus 30.5cm (12in) length of 5cm (2in) wide ribbing for the hot-water bottle cover – our sweater was for ages 7–8

► 20.5cm (8in) length of 2.5cm (1in) wide elastic

► Safety pin or bodkin, for threading the elastic

NOTE

Use a 1.25cm (½in) seam allowance

HOT-WATER BOTTLE COVER

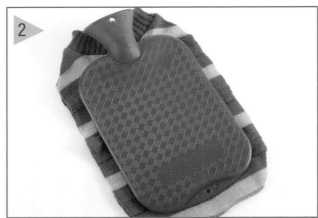

1 Firstly make sure the neck of the sweater fits over the hot-water bottle. Place the bottle centrally over the front of the sweater with the neck of the bottle just above the neckline of the sweater.

2 Cut around the hot-water bottle, through both layers, making the cut outline 2.5cm (1in) larger than the hot-water bottle and leaving the neckline intact. If you're using fabric, follow the same process, this time cutting a curve across the top of the shape where the top of the hot-water bottle is.

3 Turn the sweater inside out so the right sides are together. Sew all around the edge, leaving the top open. An overlocker/serger is ideal if you have one; if not, finish the raw edge with zigzag or overcast stitch on your sewing machine before sewing the seam. If you're using fabric, sew the ribbing piece

into a tube then sew the tube around the top curve of the cover, before sewing around the edges of the main cover.

4 Carefully snip into the seam of the neckline if you're using a sweater, or into the ribbed seamline if you are using fabric. Pop your safety pin onto one end of the elastic and thread through the gap.

5 Pull the elastic through the channel and all the way out to the opening. Sew the ends together as shown. Neatly stuff the ends into the opening then close up the gap with small hand stitches.

6 Turn the cover right side out then slip it over your hot-water bottle. Finished!

LEGWARMERS

1 Cut a straight line across the top (armhole) of each sleeve, making them as long as you can. Cut two strips of ribbing from the bottom of the sweater, each measuring 15.5cm (6in) long. Sew the short ends together to form two tubes.

2 Sew a strip of ribbing around the top of each sleeve, right sides together.

3 Fold back the ribbing. It's as easy as that!

RAG RUG

This was one of the most time-consuming projects in the book, but so worthwhile! With virtually no sewing involved, it made the perfect project for us both to make on a sunny day while sitting in the garden.

We've used a selection of fleecy garments to create a wonderfully soft rug, but be warned: everything will be covered in fluff! Jersey fabric could be used too.

We've used bright colours, but neutrals like black, white, grey and taupe would create a more sophisticated look.

Made from

One dressing gown, two blankets, two children's hoodies, one pair of adult pyjamas

FINISHED SIZE

81.5 x 63.5cm (32 x 25in)

YOU WILL NEED

► It's difficult to determine fabric requirements – we used half a dressing gown, two baby blankets, one pair of adult pyjamas and two children's hoodies. We'd suggest you find five or six items of clothing, and keep ragging until you've used them all up!

► Latch hook tool – this is very important. We bought two, so we could work from each end of the rug at the same time!

► 91.5 x 75.5cm (36 x 29in) of hessian/ burlap/jute

► Wool or tapestry needle

NOTE

Use a 1.25cm (½in) seam allowance

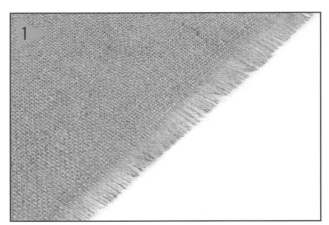

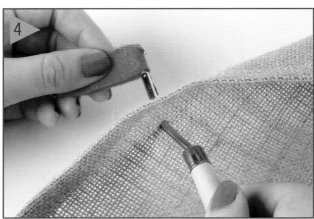

1 Find the straight grain of the hessian/burlap/jute piece. Fray the edges of the fabric by 2.5–5cm (1–2in) – don't worry too much about being exact. Cut along the frayed edges in a straight line. We will use the long, removed threads for stitching thread later, so don't throw them away – put them aside for the moment. Cut along the frayed edges in a straight line.

2 Turn over the edges once and sew with zigzag stitch to prevent fraying.

3 Cut your fabrics into 2.5 x 8cm (1 x 3in) strips.

4 Take your latch hook through the hessian/burlap/jute from the top of the fabric to the back, 4cm (1½in) from the edge. Feed a strip of fabric onto the hook.

5 Pull one end of the strip to the top.

6 Take the hook back through the hessian/burlap/jute, two or three holes away from the first, and grab the other end of the strip with the hook.

7 Pull this hooked end through to the top.

8 Two or three holes away, repeat steps 4–7 with a second strip. Don't worry about the fleece strips coming loose; they sit so closely together that they are quite secure.

9 Continue until you have covered the whole area of hessian/burlap/jute. If you're using fleece, some of the strips will stretch, so trim back the longer pieces as necessary.

10 Turn back the edge of the hessian/burlap/jute so that the bare edge of the hessian is tucked away behind the rug, approx. 5cm (2in). Sew in place with the wool or tapestry needle using the cut-away pieces of frayed hessian/burlap/jute (see step 1).

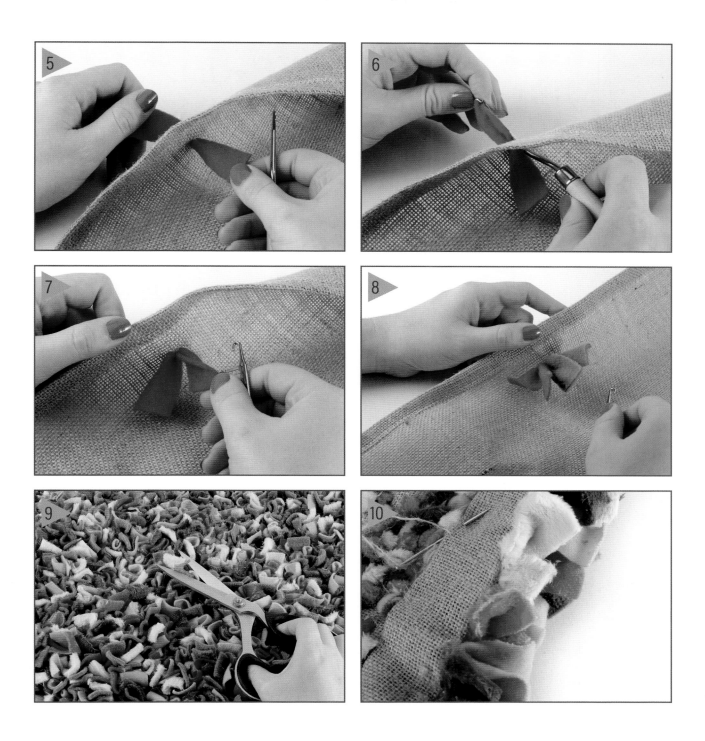

REUPHOLSTERED FOOTSTOOL

Add a new lease of life to a once-loved piece of furniture by giving it a new cover in fun, bright fabric!

We've used a dress made from spandex as we found this fabric easy to stretch around the stool; the buttons were also covered in the fabric left over. The original fringing on the stool was removed and dyed black to complement our dress fabric, so there was little waste.

Made from

One stretch-fabric dress

FINISHED SIZE

Depends on your footstool size – see the formula below

YOU WILL NEED

► Fabric requirements depend on the size of your stool; measure the top of your stool and add an extra 10–15cm (4–6in) all around for ease and seam allowances. For example, the top of ours measures 81.5 x 51cm (32 x 20in), so 91.5 x 61cm (36 x 24cm) was required, the dress we used had plenty of extra fabric

► Large staple gun and heavy-duty staples

► Strong wet fabric glue

► Satin or chalk paint, if needed

► Fringing or braid, to trim the edges

► Pincers or pliers, for removing the old cover

► Strong thread

► Optional: our stool had five covered buttons measuring 2.5cm (1in) in diameter, which we resused – buttons to cover are readily available to purchase if you need them; doll needle for attaching any buttons

NOTE

Use a 1.25cm (½in) seam allowance

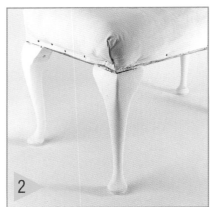

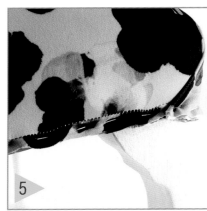

1 Remove the old cover from your stool. The cover will probably have been stapled on, so use pincers or pliers to remove them. Save any trimmings and buttons to reuse later.

2 Re-paint the legs at this point, if you wish, with satin or chalk paint suitable for use with wood.

3 Remove any zips and hardware from your garment and save them! Cut out the required amount of fabric from your garment (keep the original seams in place, if necessary) then stretch the fabric over the stool. Use lots of staples to secure. Pleat the fabric at the corners to make neat.

4 Trim the excess fabric back to the staples.

5 The staples should be quite close together and the fabric taut. Add more staples, if needed.

6 If your footstool featured buttons, carefully remove the backs and any fabric wrapped around them.

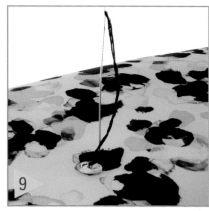

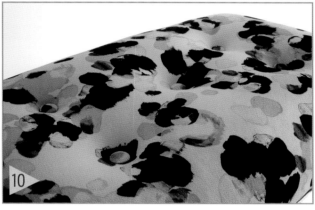

7 Cut circles from the remaining fabric that measure twice the size of each button.

8 Around the edge of one circle, make running stitches by hand. Place the top of a button in the centre of the fabric, on the wrong side, then pull the thread to gather. Press the back of the button over the top. Repeat with the remaining buttons.

9 Thread the doll needle with strong thread, take it straight through a button and down into the stool pad in the same position as the original one. If you're adding new buttons to the stool, mark four evenly spaced marks in a square approx. 13cm (5in) in from each corner, depending on the size of your stool.

10 Pull the thread tightly to create dimples in the stool, and knot on the underside of the pad. Repeat with all the remaining buttons.

11 Glue the dyed fringing or braid around the stool to conceal the staples.

Time to put your feet up!

ROPE BASKET

Create a stylish and unique rope basket that is great for storage, plants or just for decoration! This technique can also be used to make placemats or bowls. We think, once you start, you'll be hooked!

Fabric is wrapped around cord, then the cord is coiled and sewn together to make a basket. Stretch or woven fabric can be used for the wrapping fabric.

Made from

Two T-shirts, one pair of shorts, three pairs of trousers

FINISHED SIZE

22.75cm (9in) in diameter, 25.5cm (10in) tall

YOU WILL NEED

► Unwanted garments in complementary colours, or approx. 112 x 127cm (44 x 50in) fabric – we used three pairs of trousers, two tops and a pair of shorts. Try to use fabrics of the same weights

► Approx. 27.5m (30yd) of 5mm (¼in) thick cotton piping cord

► Denim sewing-machine needle

► Strong wet fabric glue

► Hand-sewing needle and strong thread

► Optional: fabric clips

1 Cut the fabric into 4cm (1½in) wide strips and in various lengths. Wrap a strip of fabric around the cord at a diagonal angle, making sure to cover it.

2 Place the second strip over the end of the first and continue wrapping. If you find it easier, glue the start and end of the fabric to keep it in place. Alternatively, you can use clips to hold the ends in place. Keep adding the fabric strips to the cord until you have approx. 27.5m (30yd). (You can always add more later, if you like – see step 5, opposite.)

3 Start curling one end of the cord into a flat coil. Once you have a 10cm (4in) circle, use a wide zigzag stitch on your sewing machine and sew the coil in place, stitching over the area where each spiral of cord meets to join them together.

4 Continue to coil and sew until you have a circle measuring 23cm (9in). The shape of the basket can be changed by altering the angle at which you sew – bowing out in the centre, narrowing at the top... the choice is yours! Don't worry about perfection; your basket will have a more organic feel if it's not quite perfect. To shape your basket, simply tilt the circle to the right and continue coiling and sewing in the same way (but at an angle) to create curved sides.

Tips

▶ If you find you have gaps in the zigzag stitching, use a little strong wet fabric glue to seal the gaps.

▶ Heavily patterned fabric will disguise any wonky stitching!

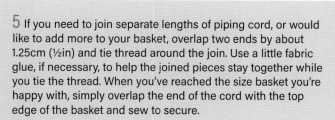

5 If you need to join separate lengths of piping cord, or would like to add more to your basket, overlap two ends by about 1.25cm (½in) and tie thread around the join. Use a little fabric glue, if necessary, to help the joined pieces stay together while you tie the thread. When you've reached the size basket you're happy with, simply overlap the end of the cord with the top edge of the basket and sew to secure.

6 To make the handles, first take two 66cm (26in) lengths of wrapped cord, coil them into separate 6.5cm (2½in) wide circles and sew with zigzag stitch.

7 Keeping a long loop shape on one side, take the end of the cord around one of the circles twice. Sew the end and loop in place with zigzag stitch. Repeat with the other handle.

8 Glue or hand sew the handles to each side of the basket.

TEA-TOWEL TOTE

You can find some beautifully illustrated tea towels in charity/thrift/op shops, and it seems quite a shame sometimes to use them for drying the dishes!

They make perfect panels for creating unique tote bags, large enough to store craft mats, rulers and, of course, shopping!

Made from

Four tea towels

FINISHED SIZE

44.5 x 48.5 x 9cm (17½ x 19 x 3½in)

YOU WILL NEED

▶ Two 2.5cm (1in) thick wooden dowels measuring (16½in) long

▶ Two linen tea towels for the outer panels, or two 101.5 x 73.5cm (40 x 29in) pieces of outer fabric – our tea towels are patterned, and measure 50.75 x 73.5cm (20 x 29in)

▶ Two coordinating tea towels for the lining pieces, or two 101.5 x 73.5cm (40 x 29in) pieces of lining fabric – ours are plain, and measure 50.75 x 73.5cm (20 x 29in)

▶ Optional: fusible interfacing (see tip on page 66)

NOTE

Use a 1.25cm (½in) seam allowance

1 Trim two outer tea towels to 48.5 x 49.5cm (19 x 19½in), or cut out two outer pieces from one of the 101.5 x 73.5cm (40 x 29in) pieces. These will be the front and back panels.

2 Cut four 6.5 x 43.5 (2½ x 17in) pieces of lining fabric for the sides.

3 Sew two strips right sides together to either side of the outer front panel, aligning the top edges. Repeat with the remaining strips on the outer back panel.

4 Use one of these outer panels as a template to cut two lining pieces to the same size and shape – unpick any hems if needed! (If your tea towels are smaller than ours, you may need to join the pieces.)

5 From the remaining outer tea towels, or the outer fabric, cut eight handle pieces (we cut four from each tea towel), each measuring 11.5 x 21.5cm (4½ x 8½in). If you don't have enough tea towel fabric, because yours are smaller than ours, you can cut eight handles from lining fabric.

6 In pairs, sew the handle pieces along the 21.5cm (8½in) sides only, right sides together, to make tubes. Turn the handles right side out and press.

Tip

If your fabric has a loose weave, try ironing fusible interfacing on the back to give it more structure!

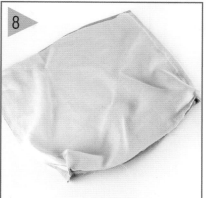

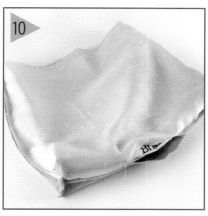

7 Fold each handle in half. On the right sides of the fabric, pin or clip the handles to the tops of the outer front and back panels, 1.25cm (½in) in from each side and facing inwards.

8 Sew the lining pieces right sides together along the sides and base, leaving the cut-out corners unsewn and a turning gap in the bottom of 15.5cm (6in). Pull the cut out corners open so that the side seams sit over the base seam, then sew across the seams to make the bag base square.

9 Sew the outer pieces right sides together in the same way, this time leaving no turning gap. Turn the outer bag right side out. Edge stitch around the side seams to help give structure to the bag.

10 Drop the outer bag inside the lining, right sides together, and sew around the top.

11 Turn the bag right side out. Sew the turning gap closed.

12 Push the lining inside the bag then edge stitch around the top.

13 Place the wooden dowels inside the handle pockets and sew just underneath and along the outside edges to prevent them from moving (see image, right) to finish.

CHILDREN'S PINAFORE DRESS

A pretty pinafore dress for your little one, made from ladies' wide-leg trousers, and no pattern needed!

Our pinafore was made for a 3-4 year old. To fit the pinafore to your own child, see 'Measurements' on page 70.

Made from

One pair of wide-leg trousers

FINISHED SIZE

See the introduction above for measuring instructions

YOU WILL NEED

▶ Pair of adult ladies' wide-leg trousers, or approx. 152.5 x 28cm (60 x 11in) of fabric – we used a pair of UK size 12 (US 10 / EU 40) ladies' trousers

▶ Two coordinating buttons

▶ Approx. 33cm (13in) length of 2.5cm (1in) wide elastic

▶ Safety pin or bodkin, for threading the elastic

NOTE

Use a 1.25cm (½in) seam allowance

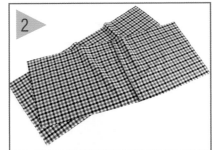

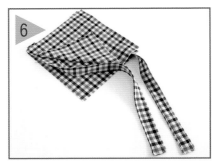

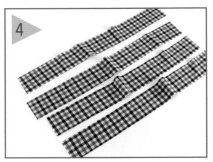

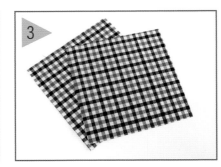

1 Cut away the hems of the trousers. Remove any zips and buttons and save them! From the bottom of each trouser leg, cut the length of the skirt plus 7.5cm (3in). Our trouser leg was 25.5cm (10in) wide, so we had a piece of fabric measuring 51cm (20in) by the length required from each leg (see 'Measurements', below right).

2 Cut away one side seam and open out the fabrics.

3 For the bib, cut two pieces of fabric from the remaining trouser fabric, each approx. 21.5cm (8½in) wide by the length you measured.

4 Cut four 4cm (1½in) wide pieces for the straps, each measuring the strap length you've measured plus 5cm (2in).

5 Sew the straps right sides together in pairs, along two sides and one end. Turn the straps the right way out and topstitch along each long edge.

6 Place the unsewn ends of the straps onto the right side of one bib piece: they should sit 1.25cm (½in) in from each side edge, the ends matching the top of the bib, and face inwards. Place the second bib over the top, its right side facing down (so the straps are sandwiched in between). Pin. Make sure the straps are tucked in between the layers, away from the side edges of the bib, as we'll be sewing these in a moment!

Measurements

With the child you're making the dress for, measure:
- ▶ the **waistband** length – this is the waist measurement
- ▶ the **skirt length** – this is from the waist to how long you want the skirt of the dress to be
- ▶ the **bib** length – this is from the waistband to the top of the chest
- ▶ the **straps** – measure from the top of the bib over one shoulder and down to the back waistband, on the opposite side of the body (as the straps are crossed over each other).

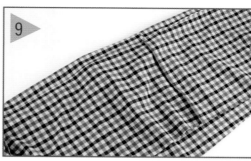

7 Sew around the top and sides of the bib, leaving the bottom open. This will secure the ends of the straps tucked between the layers. Turn the bib right side out and press.

8 Topstitch all around the bib, closing up the bottom edge in the process but without turning in this edge. Sew a buttonhole to the correct size of your button, 1.25cm (½in) away from the end of each strap.

9 Sew the skirt pieces right sides together along both side edges to make a tube. Finish the seams if you wish with an overlocker/serger, or with zigzag stitch on your sewing machine. Make a channel for the elastic by folding over the top of the skirt to the wrong side by 1.25cm (½in) then again by 3.5cm (1¼in) and sewing close to the fold.

10 Fold under the bottom of the bib by 6mm (¼in) and press. Place the bottom of the bib along the centre-top of the skirt, over the right side of the skirt and with the top of the skirt matching the raw bottom edge of the fold. Sew two rows of stitches to secure, concealing the raw edge of the bib in between the two rows.

11 Unpick a few stitches at the top of both side seams on the skirt back to access the channel for the elastic. Attach a safety pin to one end of the elastic and thread it all the way through the channel, keeping hold of the other end. Bring it out again on the other side, as shown. Pull the elastic to gather the skirt; if possible, secure the gather temporarily with a safety pin or a few hand stitches and have the child try the dress on for size.

12 Once you are happy with the fit (trimming the elastic as necessary), sew the ends together, remove the safety pin or hand stitches and carefully push the end of the elastic inside the channel. Sew the gap closed.

13 Sew two buttons to the back of the waistband, 7.5cm (3in) each side of the centre point on the skirt back.

14 Turn the hem up twice by 1.25cm (½in) and sew. Press to finish your lovely pinafore.

SMOCKED STORAGE BAG

Smocking is a way of pinching, pleating and stitching fabric to create pattern and texture. The type of smocking in this project is sometimes called 'Canadian smocking', and is a technique often used in pillow-cover and homeware designs. Usually, it involves drawing a grid on the wrong side of the fabric and marking which squares are to be sewn; for this project we're using a checked shirt, so the grid is already there!

Smocking can be quite time-consuming, but having just a couple of rows of smocking at the top of the bag makes this a quick project to sew and a great introduction to the technique if it is new to you.

Make sure the checks are woven, not printed; with a woven check you can guarantee the squares will be straight. The checks on this shirt measure approximately 4cm (1½in) square. The finished size of the bag is 34.5 x 23cm (13½ x 9in), which uses the largest single piece of fabric that could be cut from the back of the shirt. It could be made bigger by joining fabric together before smocking. The size of your bag will vary if your checks are larger or smaller than ours.

Made from

One pillowcase, one shirt

FINISHED SIZE

34.5cm x 23 x 7.5cm (13½ x 9 x 3in)

YOU WILL NEED

▶ Large men's checked shirt, or 69 x 40.5cm (27 x 16in) piece of checked fabric

▶ 69 x 28cm (27 x 11in) piece of lining fabric – we used the second of our pair of pillowcases from the Tweed Tote (see page 32) as the lining

▶ 10 buttons

▶ Hand-sewing needle and strong coordinating thread

▶ Optional: thimble

NOTE

Use a 1.25cm (½in) seam allowance

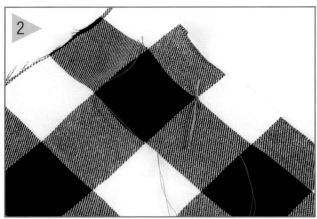

1 Cut a length of fabric measuring 69 x 28cm (27 x 11in). We're going to smock the black squares, so make sure there is a contrast square at each side (adjust your fabric measurements slightly, if necessary).

2 Starting in one corner, take your needle through each corner of one black square in order, catching a couple of threads of fabric.

3 Pull the thread tight to gather all four corners together. Knot the thread tightly then cut away the excess. We've used red thread deliberately so that you can see the stitches; we recommend using a matching thread for smocking.

4 Repeat across one short end of the fabric, completing two rows of black squares.

5 Do the same on the opposite short end of the fabric.

6 Sew buttons over the smocked points of the second row. Although we have black buttons from our shirt that we could have used, we thought it would be fun to raid the button jar and add colourful buttons instead! Beads would also work well.

7 From the remaining fabric, cut two pieces – one measuring 56 x 11.5cm (22 x 4½in) and one measuring 13 x 11.5cm (5 x 4½in).

8 Fold the long sides of each to the centre, then fold in half again and press. Edge stitch along each side.

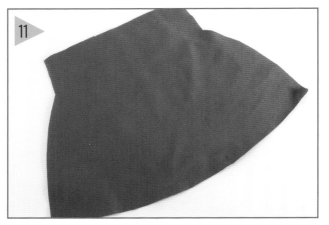

9 Fold each strip in half then sew one to the centre-top of one smocked end of fabric, and the other to the centre-top of the opposite end, both loops facing inwards. The raw ends of the long strap should sit on top of each other, and the ends of the short strap sit side by side.

10 Fold the fabric in half with the smocked ends together. Place the folded bag panel over two layered pieces of lining fabric then arrange the bag panel fabric so that it is symmetrical. On the lining, draw around the edge of the folded outer bag, adding 1.25cm (½in) extra to the bottom.

11 Cut out the shapes.

12 Sew the lining pieces right sides together, leaving the top open and a turning gap of about 10cm (4in) in the base. Pinch the corners so that the side seams sit over the base seam and create 'triangles'. Measure 4cm (1½in) from the points and sew straight across the triangles. This will make the bag base square.

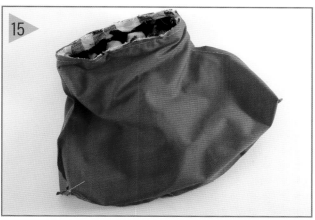

13 Cut away the excess fabric at the corners. Repeat to sew the sides of the outer bag, this time leaving no turning gap.

14 Turn the outer bag right side out.

15 Drop the outer bag inside the lining, right sides together. Sew around the top, matching the side seams. Be careful not to sew over the points of your smocking!

16 Turn the bag right side out and sew the turning gap closed.

17 Push the lining inside the bag and press. Thread the long handle through the shorter one, then your bag is finished!

TABLECLOTH CURTAINS

Tablecloths are perfect for so many projects as they are just large pieces of fabric! The tie-tops for our curtains means there is no need for curtain hooks or rails, too.

Choose a heavy-weight cloth for an unlined curtain. Shop around the thrift stores to find the largest size available, too. You will also need a curtain pole slightly wider than your window.

Our window measures 91.5 x 119.5cm (36 x 47in), and we wanted the curtains to be a little longer. Generally, if you're making two curtains, the fabric width of each curtain is the width of the whole window, or even a little wider. You may need to join fabrics for an extra-large window.

Made from

Tablecloth

1 From the tablecloth, cut out eight pieces of fabric each measuring 18 x 79cm (7 x 31in).

2 Fold each piece in half lengthways. Trim the ends at a 45-degree angle then sew together around the raw edges, leaving a turning gap in the long side of about 7.5cm (3in).

3 Turn the pieces right side out then hand-sew the opening closed with matching thread.

4 Cut the remaining fabric into two rectangles – the width of each should be the width of your window plus 2.5cm (1in) for seam allowances. Each of our rectangles measured 86.25 x 157.5cm (34 x 62in). We managed to use the existing hem on the tablecloth on two sides of the curtain; if this isn't possible with yours, turn over the raw edges twice by 1.25cm (½in) and sew to hem. Fold the ties in half then pin them evenly along the tops of the curtains – four to each curtain – with the fold of the ties sitting 2.5cm (1in) down from the top edge. Sew in place. Tie them around the curtain pole to finish.

TIE-DYE BEAN BAG

Tie dyeing is so much fun, and it is a simple way to transform a plain coloured fabric into something unique! Tie-dye kits are an affordable way of dyeing, as they usually include protective gloves, aprons and table coverings. There are many different techniques, you can use: we liked the starburst effect but rainbow stripes would work just as well for this bean bag too!

Made from

Bedsheet

FINISHED SIZE
34.25 x 22.75 x 7.5cm (13½ x 9 x 3in)

YOU WILL NEED

▶ Single/twin bed sheet made from 100% cotton, or 112 x 165cm (44 x 65in) of 100% cotton fabric – it's important that you use cotton, as this is the best for dyeing

▶ Tie-dye kit – our kit contained fifteen 5g (¼oz) sachets of dye powder and fifteen 100ml (3½ fl oz) squirt bottles. We used six different colours (orange, yellow, green, purple, pink and blue), so six sachets, but you could use more or fewer shades if you prefer

▶ Elastic bands

▶ Rubber gloves

▶ 46cm (18in) zip

▶ 5kg (5 cu ft) of bean-bag filling in a stockinette bag – keep an eye out for ones made from eco-friendly materials!

▶ 25.5cm (10in) diameter plate or a large curved object, to use as a circle template

▶ Zipper foot

▶ Optional: fabric glue pen

NOTE
Use a 1.25cm (½in) seam allowance

80

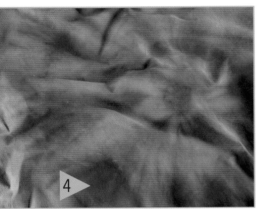

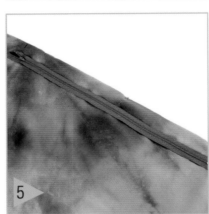

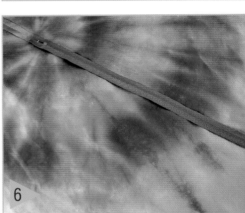

1 Trim away any elastic if your sheet is fitted. Wash the fabric, and cover your working surface with a protective cover. Once the fabric is washed, and while it is still wet, from the centre twist the whole sheet into a spiral.

2 Tie three elastic bands around the spiral to divide the fabric into six sections.

3 Mix up the dye colours and squirt over each section on both sides of the spiralled fabric. Make sure you wear protective rubber gloves!

4 Leave the fabric overnight so the dye can develop. Undo the bands, rinse the fabric until the water runs clear, dry it and then press.

5 Cut one piece of fabric measuring 81.5 x 112cm (32 x 44in) and two pieces each measuring 42 x 112cm (16½ x 44in). Take notice of where the starbust effect sits on your fabric; you may be able to position it in the centre of the bean bag. Pin the two narrower pieces right sides together along one long side, then place the zip along this edge, 20.5cm (8in) up from the short bottom end. Within the seam allowance, mark the fabric just inside the points where the metal zip stops sit.

6 From the short bottom end, sew up to the first mark with your sewing machine's regular stitch length. Reverse a couple of stitches then sew between the two marks on your longest stitch length. Finish the rest of the seam on your regular stitch length, again reversing a couple of stitches at the start. Press the seam open, place the zip over the seam and secure with a fabric glue pen. (You could tack/baste the zip temporarily in place by hand if you prefer.)

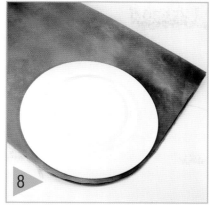

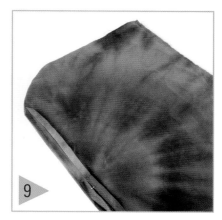

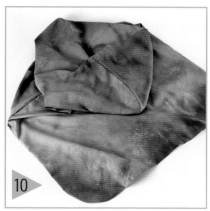

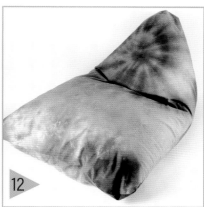

7 Sew all around the zip, then unpick the long stitches over the zip.

8 Place the stitched panel and the 81.5 x 112cm (32 x 44in) piece of fabric right sides together. Fold in half lengthways. Use your circle template to cut a curve from the bottom-left corner (this is the corner not on the fold).

9 Open out the panels again and sew, leaving the straight top end open. Pull the top open and match the side seams in the centre; the zip should now be at the side. Fold the whole panel in half again and curve the corner.

10 Open out the panel once more then sew around the top; make sure the zip is open before you do this!

11 Turn the bean-bag cover right side out and stuff your bean filling inside.

12 Fold the cover as you stuff to ensure you have a raised head section. Finished!

Tip

Tie dyeing is fun for the kids to do, too – let them loose on some old
T-shirts and see what they come up with!
Be aware: this could be messy...

UPCYCLED ARMCHAIR COVER

One of our favourite projects in this book: updating a tired old armchair with jeans! Although it took quite a few pairs of jeans to cover, it worked out to be much more affordable than buying upholstery fabric. If you don't want to use denim, look for heavy fabric such as curtain material or canvas.

On this occasion, a bit of stretch in the denim was beneficial to help the cover fit snugly around the chair. We managed to salvage the seat cushion and the zip.

It's worth investing in a few tools to help remove the old cover without damaging it, such as pincers or pliers and a staple lifter. You'll also need a staple gun to re-apply the cover.

Made from

Five pairs of jeans

FINISHED SIZE

35.5 x 35.5 x 38cm (14 x 14 x 15in)

YOU WILL NEED

▶ Fabric requirements may differ, depending on the size of your armchair – we used five pairs of large men's jeans, or approx. 152.5 x 203.5cm (60 x 80in) fabric

▶ Tools for reupholstering – we recommend pincers or pliers, a staple lifter and a staple gun

▶ Long zip, for your cushion pad cover – you may be able to salvage the old zip; if not, measure the width of your cushion pad and then subtract 10cm (4in) to work out the approximate length zip you'll need

▶ Optional: a scrubbing brush, for distressing the fabric

NOTE

Use the same seam allowance used for the original cover

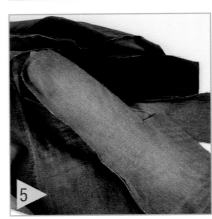

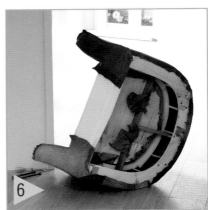

1 Carefully remove the old cover. You will probably have to take off the legs of the chair. Take note (and pictures, if it helps) of how the original cover was attached to the chair, as this can differ from chair to chair. Try to save any zips and linings to reuse later. Our chair's original cover had 10 panels on the front and two on the back; there were also five panels for the seat cushion pad – two either side of the zip, one for the gusset and two for the front and back. Carefully unpick each panel. It's a good idea to number each piece, particularly if there are a lot of panels as we had with our chair!

2 Cut your jeans into the largest pieces you can, then use the removed cover pieces as templates to trim the denim strips to their shapes. Again, number the denim pieces (this time on the back). As the two original back panels were quite large, we worked out that we needed to join several denim pieces together.

3 Sew the front panel pieces together in the same order as the removed cover, using the same seam allowances as the original cover. We decided to sew the front strips wrong sides together and fray the seams for effect.

4 Sew the back panel strips of denim right sides together.

5 Fold both the front and back sections in half then crease the centre tops. With the front and back sections right sides together, and matching the centre marks, sew the top of the back to the top of the front. With right sides together, sew in the end/arm panels.

6 Try your cover on for size. At this point you can take in the seams to make the fit more snug, if needed. Once you are happy with the fit, pull the fabric tightly over the chair and staple around the bottom.

Tip

Use a small stitch on your sewing machine to make the seams strong; they will be under a lot of pressure when the cover is stretched over the chair.

7 Use plenty of staples, pulling the fabric as tight as you can. Here's the chair back shown from the back...

8 ... and here it is shown from the front. Finish the cover by covering the seat section, securing the panel from the back of the chair then pulling it right underneath the base of the chair at the front.

9 Replace the base of the chair (see the removed base in step 6, opposite), reattaching the feet if necessary.

10 Take one of the new denim zip panels and sew it to one side of the salvaged (or new) zip, right sides together. Press. Repeat on the other side of the zip with the other zip panel.

11 Sew the zip panel to the gusset piece, right sides together, to make a 'loop' of fabric – as with the chair back, we had to join several pieces of denim together to make up the gusset. Sew the loop to the seat cushion front, right sides together.

12 With the zip open, sew in the seat cushion back right sides together. Push the original cushion pad inside then pull the zip closed.

13 If you wish, fray the raw edges of the front of the armchair – a scrubbing brush may help! Ready to relax?

TWO-TONED PIPED PILLOW

This pillow cover is made from the leftover shirt pieces from the Tumbling-block Pillow (see page 16), plus a few strips of the striped trousers from the Patchwork Throw (see page 24). The placket on the shirt was particularly interesting, so we saved it to use as a feature fastening on the front of the cushion. The buttons were also salvaged from one of the shirts.

Piping is an effective way of finishing off a project. Our piping was made with random lengths of cut-offs, so even the smallest scrap didn't go to waste!

Made from

Three shirts, one pair of trousers

FINISHED SIZE

43.5cm (17in) square

YOU WILL NEED

▶ 43.5cm (17in) square pillow pad

▶ 44.5 x 28cm (17½ x 11in) pale fabric, for the front

▶ 44.5 x 20.5cm (17½ x 8in) contrast fabric, for the front – ours included the shirt placket; if your piece doesn't feature a placket, you will need to cut a piece of fabric measuring 44.5 x 23cm (17½ x 9in)

▶ 44.5cm (17½in) square of fabric, for the back

▶ 4.5cm (1¾in) wide strips of fabric for piping, enough to sew together and make a long strip measuring 205cm (80in) in length

▶ 6mm (¼in) wide piping cord, approx. 188cm (74in) in length

▶ Buttons – we used five, but if you are using a shirt placket you will need to match the buttons to the buttonholes

▶ Zipper foot

NOTE

Use a 5mm (¼in) seam allowance

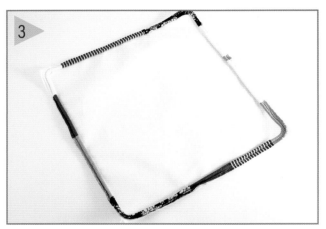

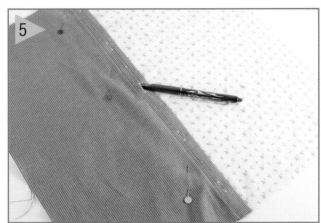

1 Join the strips right sides together along the short ends. Press the seams open.

2 Wrap the long, joined strip around the piping cord and sew in place, close to the cord (a zipper foot will help with this). Trim the seam allowance back to 5mm (¼in).

3 Sew the piping raw edges together to the back of the cushion cover. (See technique on page 15.)

4 Take the pale fabric piece, fold one 44.5cm (17½in) edge over twice by 1.25cm (½in) and sew to hem.

5 Take the contrast fabric for the front. If you're not using a shirt placket, fold the 44.5cm (17½in) edge over twice by 1.25cm (½in), mark the position of three evenly spaced buttonholes and sew. (As we used an existing placket, we had five buttonholes.) Place the two front sections together, the contrast fabric (buttonhole) side on top of and overlapping the pale fabric, and the two fabrics facing up. Adjust the front layers until they form a 44.5cm (17½in) square. Pin. Use an erasable marker pen to mark the position of the buttons, through the contrast fabric's buttonholes and on to the pale fabric.

6 Carefully fold back the contrast fabric piece and sew the buttons onto the pale fabric piece, over the markings. (You may need to remove a few pins to do this.) Button up the cushion front. Sew the front to the piped backing piece, right sides together. Open up the buttons and turn the pillow cover right side out. Insert your cushion pad and you're finished! Here's the pillow from the back.

WOVEN DENIM TOTE

Fabric weaving is great fun, and with it many different effects can be achieved. For this bag, we created quite an illusional effect. We also left the edges raw, so that the fabric would fray a little over time. If you prefer, you could stitch along the raw edges after weaving.

We've used denim for our tote, but you could use other strong fabrics such as canvas, khaki or curtain fabric.

Made from

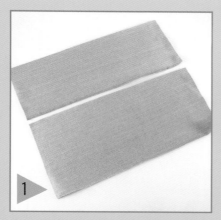

Two pairs of jeans, one pillowcase

FINISHED SIZE

37 x 39.5cm (14½ x 15½in)

YOU WILL NEED

▶ Two pairs of jeans, one dark and one light – if you're using alternative fabrics, you'll need two 45.75 x 40.75cm (18 x 16in) pieces of contrast fabric for the bag front; three pieces of dark fabric and three pieces of light fabric for the bag back, each measuring 38 x 7.5cm (15 x 3in); and two dark and two light fabrics for the handle, each measuring 10 x 30.5cm (4 x 12in)

▶ Strong wet fabric glue

▶ 76.25 x 35.5cm (30 x 14in) piece of lining fabric – an old pillowcase is perfect!

▶ 86.25 x 40.5cm (34 x 16in) piece of single-sided fusible foam stabilizer

▶ Fabric marker pen and ruler

▶ Mat or board and tape, to secure the fabric when weaving

▶ Optional: 41 x 38cm (16 x 15in) piece of lightweight fusible interfacing (see step 9)

NOTE

Use a 1.25cm (½in) seam allowance

1 You'll need a piece of light denim measuring 41 x 38cm (16 x 15in). The largest pieces of our denim were from the thigh sections, and we needed to join two pieces measuring 41 x 20.5cm (16 x 8in) and 40.75 x 18cm (16 x 7in) to make up the overall quantity needed.

2 If you have to join two pieces of fabric like we did, cut two strips of fabric, each measuring 38 x 6.5cm (15 x 2½in), and sew to each side of the two pieces. This is simply to hold the fabrics together when weaving. If you managed to cut the 41 x 38cm (16 x 15in) piece in one, this stage is not necessary.

3 Fold the panel in half widthways. Draw lines from the fold, starting where the two fabrics meet (or in the centre if you're using one piece of fabric) and finishing at the edge. Drawing these lines at an angle, as we have, will give your woven bag front a nice distorted effect! Make these lines further apart as you reach the top and bottom of the fabric, too.

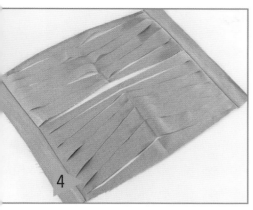

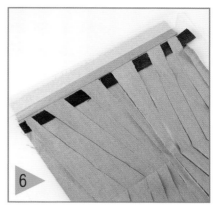

4 With the fabric still folded, cut along these lines, stopping at the border strips. If you're using one piece of fabric, stop 5mm (¼in) from the edge. Open out the fabric.

5 Cut out fifteen 2.5 x 41cm (1 x 16in) strips of dark denim.

6 Place the cut panel from step 4 over your mat or board and tape the top to it to hold the panel in place. Weave the first strip over and under the cuts in the panel, then push the strip right to the top.

7 Weave the second strip through the cut panel, this time weaving under then over. Push this up until it butts against the first strip.

8 Continue until the whole panel has been woven. Add a spot of wet glue under some of the overlapping fabric pieces to hold them in place.

9 If you're going to sew along the raw edges of the strips, do so now – we're leaving our denim to fray. If you sew the raw edges, it's a good idea to fuse a piece of lightweight interfacing to the wrong side to hold the strips in place. Otherwise, just fuse the foam stablizer to the wrong side. Trim the woven panel all around to measure 38 x 35.5cm (15 x 14in). Sew around all four sides within the seam allowance to secure the ends of the strips.

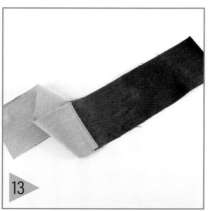

10 For the back of the bag, and if you haven't cut out your back pieces already, cut three strips each of dark and light denim measuring 38 x 7.5cm (15 x 3in). Sew the strips right sides together and alternately, taking a 1cm (⅜in) seam allowance and making a stripy effect. Press the seams open. Fuse foam to the wrong side of the back panel. Edge stitch along the seams.

11 If you wish, you can reuse a pocket from the jeans! Cut a pocket from one of the pairs of jeans. Position it on the right side of the back panel so it is 10cm (4in) down from the top and 7.5cm (3in) in from the right-hand side.

12 Cut a 2.5cm (1in) square from each bottom corner of both bag panels. Trim one panel if you need to, so both are the same size.

13 For the handles, if you haven't already, cut two dark and two light pieces of denim each measuring 10 x 30.5cm (4 x 12in). Sew a dark to a light piece across one short end, right sides together. Press the seams open. Repeat.

14 Take one handle piece and fold the long edges to the centre and press.

15 Fold the whole handle in half and press again. Edge stitch all the way around. Repeat for the other handle.

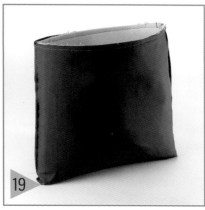

16 Position a handle onto the right side of a bag panel, placing the handle ends 13cm (5in) in from the side edges and 13cm (5in) down from the top. The handle on the back of the bag should tuck slightly into the pocket. Sew the ends in place by stitching a box shape.

17 To make the lining, cut two pieces of fabric each measuring 38 x 35.5cm (15 x 14in). Cut a 2.5cm (1in) square from each bottom corner. Sew the lining panels right sides together, leaving the top and cut-out corners unsewn and a turning gap in the base of about 10cm (4in). Open out the cut-out corners, so that the side seams sit over the base seam, and sew straight across the seams to square the bag base. Leave the lining inside out.

18 Sew the outer bag together in the same way, this time omitting the turning gap in the base. Turn the bag right side out and push out the corners.

19 Drop the outer bag inside the lining, right sides together and matching the seams. Sew around the top.

20 Turn the whole bag right side out and sew the turning gap closed by hand or machine.

21 Push the lining inside the bag and edge stitch around the top. One final press and you're ready to go!

≫ INDEX ≪

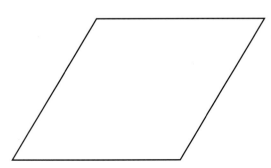

TUMBLING-BLOCK
PILLOW

Diamond template

(see page 16)